Ways We Go to School

written by **Jay Dale**

Some children go to school on a *bus*.

Look at the children.

They are going to school on a big yellow bus.

The bus will take them all the way to school.

3

Some children go to school on a *train*.

Look at this boy and his sister.
They go to school every day by train.

Some children go to school on a *streetcar*.

6

A streetcar is like a train, but it is not as long. This streetcar goes up and down the *street*— all the way to school.

Some children go to school on a *bike*.

This boy is going
to school on his bike.
He puts on his bike *helmet*
and rides along the *path*.
He has to look out
for people.

Some children go to school in a *car*.

This girl is going to school with her dad.

There are lots of cars at school.

She has to look out for them!

Some children go to school on a *boat*.

This boat is also called a ferry.

It is fun to go to school on a ferry.

The *waves* push the ferry up and down!

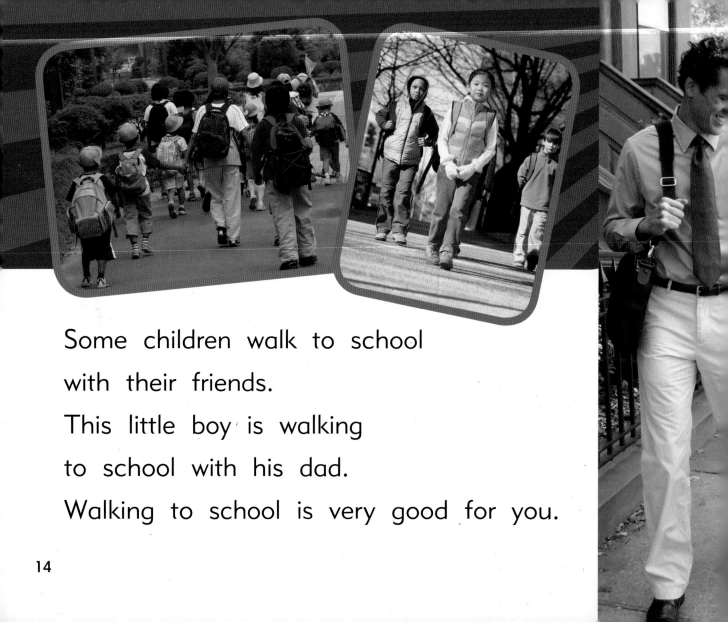

Some children walk to school
with their friends.
This little boy is walking
to school with his dad.
Walking to school is very good for you.

Do you go to school:

on a bus?

on a train?

on a streetcar?

on a bike?

in a car?

on a ferry?

Or do you walk to school?

Picture Glossary

bike

car

street

streetcar

boat

helmet

train

bus

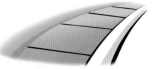

path

waves